By Tony Tallarico

Copyright © 1991 Kidsbooks Inc. and Tony Tallarico
7004 N. California Ave.
Chicago, IL. 60645

ANSWERS ON LAST PAGE

Can you find at least <u>ten</u> things in this picture that start with the letter *L?*

3

Help Lisa find the following objects hidden in space:

Apple
Cup
Elephant
Football
Ghost
Hats (2)
Ice skate
Pencil
Pig
Pumpkin
Rabbit
Television set

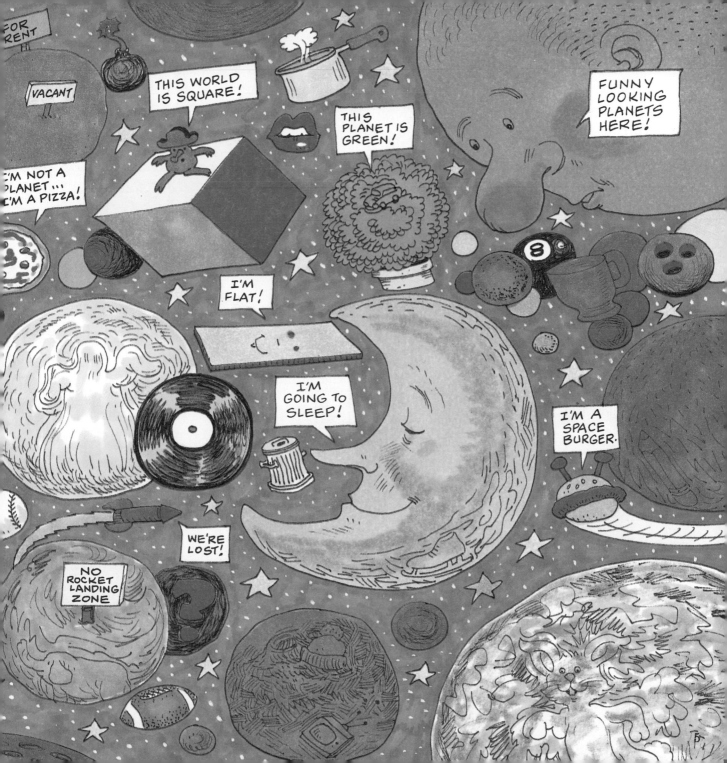

One day, Lisa was going to meet a friend. She turned the corner and suddenly... a wacky maze appeared! Help Lisa find her friend by going through the maze correctly, while finding lots of things along the way.

FIND A DINOSAUR
THEN CONTINUE

FIND 5 BALLOONS
THEN CONTINUE

FIND 3 PENCILS
THEN CONTINUE

FIND ONE HORSE
THEN CONTINUE

FIND ONE UMBRELL
THEN CONTINUE

START

FIND
3 STARS
THEN
CONTINUE

FIND
4 KITES
THEN
CONTINUE

FIND
5 FISH
THEN
CONTINUE

FIND
6 FLOWERS
THEN
CONTINUE

HI, LISA!

7

Lisa had her photograph taken, but something was wrong with the camera. Can you find at least <u>seven</u> things that are different between the real Lisa and her photo?

Lisa is looking for her twin. Can you find her? Then find the twins of some of the other characters in this scene.

PLAY THE LISA TOSS GAME

1. Place the opened book on the floor about five feet away.
2. Each player gets to toss three coins at the open book.
3. Whenever a player's coin lands on an area that has a picture of Lisa, the player receives one point.
4. The first player to get 12 points is the winner.
5. Be careful. There are "take-away" point zones.
6. Have fun!

12

All the letters of the alphabet have been hidden in this wacky picture. Help Lisa find them.

"Lisa," "Lisa," "Lisa," is everywhere. Can you find Lisa's name at least <u>13</u> times in this scene?

Lisa is looking for
the following objects
at the Lost and Found
department:

Baby bottle
Clock
Clothes hanger
Footballs (2)
Jump rope
Log
Mitten
Necktie
Pillow
Sailboat
Scooter
Shovels (2)
Straw
Tree
Whistle

Help her find them.

18

Lisa is in a big department store. What's wrong here? Help Lisa find at least <u>ten</u> things that are wrong with this picture.

21

Lisa is shopping for a new blouse. Help Lisa get to the store that has the blouse on sale by leading her through the path numbers that add up to exactly 20.

23

ANSWERS

2-3

4-5

6-7

8-9

10-11

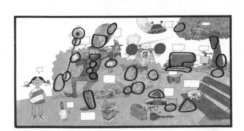

14-15

16-17

18-19

20-21

22-23